Local Agenda 21 - the process of developing local policies for sustainable development and building partnerships between local authorities and other sectors to implement them - is a crucial part of the move towards sustainability.

Local Agenda 21 is a continuing process rather than a single event, document or activity. There is no standard 'tick list' of things you must do for Local Agenda 21. Rather, the process can involve a range of activities, tools and approaches from which a local authority and its partners can choose according to local priorities and circumstances.

This booklet has been produced by the Local Agenda 21 UK Steering Group to explain what Local Agenda 21 is and through it to help local authorities and their partners work towards sustainable development in their own areas.

Each local authority will have to make careful choices about what it can realistically tackle in the short term - particularly given the current restrictions on local government powers and funding and the pressures of reorganisation, competitive tendering and other management changes. Priorities should be guided by local circumstances, needs and opportunities.

Many components of the process will already be happening in your local authority and with your community: it is not all new. The key is to recognise old and new measures as part of this new sustainable development agenda and to link global and local issues. Local Agenda 21 is where they meet.

CONTENTS

CONTENTS

CONTEXT AND ORIGINS OF LOCAL AGENDA 21

The new agenda of sustainable development

In 1987 the World Commission on Environment and Development ('the Brundtland Commission') defined sustainable development as:

"Development which meets the needs of the present without compromising the ability of future generations to meet their own needs".

Sustainable development brings together four sets of values - environmental protection, providing for the future, quality of life and fairness - to create a new policy agenda which integrates environmental, developmental, social and economic concerns. Some of its key points are:

• Safeguarding the environment is a precondition of development - not an obstacle to it. They are not alternatives, or opposites, but interdependent;

• The physical `carrying capacity' of the environment imposes limits to many human activities. We must live within these so that we pass the planet on to our descendants with its ability to support human life undamaged;

• Human wellbeing has social, cultural, moral and spiritual dimensions as well as material. Development worthy of the name must seek to support all of these, not some at the expense of others;

• All people (and all peoples) must have opportunities to develop (which does not mean that everyone should follow the same path of development);

• Development and economic growth are quite different things. It is possible to have either without the other. Development should be the primary aim of policy;

• We need broader indicators than economic growth by which to measure development.

Rio and Agenda 21

In 1992, at the UN Conference on Environment and Development (`the Earth Summit') in Rio, over 150 nations including the UK endorsed a 500 - page document, Agenda 21, which sets out how both developed and developing countries can work towards sustainable development.

Agenda 21 says that sustainable development requires humanity to:

• Reduce our use of energy and raw materials, and production of pollution and wastes;

• Protect fragile ecosystems;

• Share wealth, opportunities and responsibilities more fairly between North and South, between countries, and between different social groups within each country, with special emphasis on the needs and rights of the poor and disadvantaged.

Agenda 21 also argues that we will only be able to achieve these aims through planned, democratic, cooperative processes:

• We will not achieve sustainable development by accident but must consciously plan and work for it, at all levels from international to local;

• All people, including poor and disadvantaged groups, must have a say in decisions about environment and development;

• All social groups and interests, including business, education, and voluntary and community groups as well as governments at all levels, will need to work in partnership.

Local government and sustainable development

Agenda 21 singles out local government as having a special role. Two thirds of the actions in Agenda 21 require the active involvement of local authorities. Chapter 28 of Agenda 21 calls on them to initiate Local Agenda 21 processes - partnerships for sustainable development at a local level - by 1996. Local Agenda 21 is about applying the partnership approach to achieve action for sustainable development at local level.

Local Agenda 21 is related to a range of other sustainable development initiatives:

•   The United Nations has set up a Commission for Sustainable Development (CSD) whose job is to encourage and help governments to implement Agenda 21;

•   Agenda 21 asks governments to report annually to the CSD on their actions to promote sustainable development. The UK government has produced 'Sustainable Development: the UK strategy' in response. It confirms the government's support for Local Agenda 21.

•   The European Union has adopted its Fifth Environmental Action Programme, whose subtitle is 'Towards Sustainability'. Like Agenda 21 it argues for reducing resource and energy use and wastes, and for a partnership approach. It insists that environmental considerations must be integrated into other policies - especially those for energy, industry, transport, agriculture and tourism - rather than treated separately. The Fifth Programme also strongly emphasises 'subsidiarity', in the sense of delegation of decisions to the most local level possible (not only from the European Union to national governments).

•   The International Council for Local Environmental Initiatives (ICLEI) drafted Chapter 28 of Agenda 21 and coordinated the local government input to the Earth Summit and the follow-up to Rio, and has produced guidelines for Local Agenda 21. ICLEI is now developing a 'Local Agenda 21 model programme' which includes 21 local authorities from both Southern and Northern hemispheres.

Local Agenda 21 in the UK

In the UK, all the local authority Associations have joined in setting up a Local Agenda 21 Steering Group representing industry, trades unions, the voluntary sector, womens'

organisations and higher education as well as local government. The Associations have asked the Local Government Management Board, under the direction of the Steering Group, to coordinate and drive Local Agenda 21 on their behalf by:

•   Publishing guidance (including this booklet)

•   Organising conferences and roundtable discussions on aspects of sustainable development at a local level;

•   Representing the interests of local government in national and international policy, for example in contributions to the National Sustainable Development Strategy, the European Commission and direct to the CSD;

•   Appointing a Local Agenda 21 Project Officer to work with local authorities.

Many local authorities have already taken major steps. Local Agenda 21 is increasingly recognised as:

•   An important acknowledgement of the role of local government in the sustainable development process;

•   A moral responsibility (although not a statutory duty);

•   The logical next stage in many local authorities' policies and programmes;

•   A way to bring together, and mutually strengthen, an authority's commitments to the environment, to local economic and social development, and to local democracy.

Integrating sustainable development aims into the local authority's policies and activities

- Green housekeeping

- Land use planning

- Transport policies and programmes

- Economic development

- Tendering and purchaser/provider splits

- Housing services

- Tourism and visitor strategies

- Health strategies

- Welfare, equal opportunities and poverty strategies

- Explicitly 'environmental' services

Awareness raising and education

- Support for environmental education

- Awareness-raising events

- Visits and talks

- Support for voluntary groups

- Publication of local information

- Press releases

- Initiatives to encourage behaviour change and practical action

Managing and improving the local authority's own environmental performance

- Corporate commitment

- Staff training and awareness raising

- Environmental management systems

- Environmental budgeting

- Policy integration across sectors

ACTION WITHIN THE LOCAL AUTHORITY

Partnerships

- Meetings, workshops and conferences

- Working groups / advisory groups

- Round Tables

- Environment City Model

- Partnership initiatives

- Developing-world partnerships and support

Measuring, monitoring and reporting on progress towards sustainability

- Environmental monitoring

- Local state of the environment reporting

- Sustainability indicators

- Targets

- Environmental Impact Assessment (EIA)

- Strategic environmental assessment

Consulting and involving the general public

- Public consultation processes

- Fora

- Focus groups

- 'Planning for real'

- Parish Maps

- Feedback mechanisms

THE KEY ELEMENTS OF LOCAL AGENDA 21

Action within the local authority

Local authorities are major players in the local economy, manage or control important aspects of the local environment, and can strongly influence the environmental behaviour of others. Any authority can make an important contribution to local sustainability simply by setting its own house in order, continually improving its environmental performance, and leading by example. Two kinds of 'internal' activity can help with this: managing and improving the local authority's own environmental performance; integrating sustainable development aims into the local authority's policies and activities.

Many components of the process will already be happening in your local authority and with your community: it is not all new. The key is to recognise old and new measures as part of this new sustainable development agenda and to link global and local issues. Local Agenda 21 is where they meet.

Managing and improving the local authority's own environmental performance

Corporate commitment by both members and officers is an essential starting point. A clear statement of the authority's commitment provides the momentum needed to progress initiatives within the authority and puts sustainability on the agenda of other organisations in the area.

To achieve this, authorities can:

• Develop their own statements of commitment, for example through adopting an Environmental Charter or Mission Statement on sustainable development;

• Make a commitment to implement Friends of the Earth's Environmental Charter for Local Government (still highly valid four years after its launch);

• Endorse the UK Local Government Declaration on Sustainable Development;

• Adopt a corporate Sustainable Development Strategy;

• Make a commitment to work towards Local Agenda 21.

Staff training and awareness raising on environmental and sustainability issues is essential to give officers the commitment, the understanding, the techniques and the confidence to progress these matters. Local voluntary groups can help with this.

Environmental Management Systems such as Eco-Management and Audit (EMA) and BS7750 can provide a structured, explicit framework for:

• Identifying the authority's major impacts on the environment - both actual and potential (what many authorities have previously called an Environmental Audit);

• Deciding what the authority's overall aims and values are with respect to these impacts (cor responding to an Environmental Charter);

• Committing the authority to actions to imple ment the policy, with measurable targets for both activities and their results (corresponding to many authorities' Environmental Action Plans);

• Specifying who is going to carry out the actions, with what resources, over what time, and how implementation and progress are to be monitored (an area where previous practice has often fallen down);

• Having progress assessed independently, reporting on it to the public, and updating the policy and programme as needed.

This approach uses methods that many local authorities have already been developing but, crucially, makes them explicit and fills many of the gaps. The disciplines it provides - especially setting targets, allocating responsibilities and resources, and monitoring and reporting progress - can help authorities implement all the environmental actions suggested in this booklet.

Environmental budgeting. Environmental actions always involve costs and/or savings in one way or another. Budgetary processes should:

- Allow extra expenditure to be argued for on environmental grounds (which does not mean every bid will succeed!);

- Provide mechanisms for 'upfront' investments, for example in energy saving, to be funded and justified by the expected future savings;

- Give all departments an incentive to achieve savings through environmental efficiency - for example by allowing them to use some of the savings themselves;

- Include environmental performance in performance indicators and criteria for assessing the quality of service delivery and value for money.

Policy integration across sectors. Decision making processes need to ensure that each service function takes account of environmental consequences in other areas. For example:

- Decisions on the centralisation or decentralisation of services need to recognise the impacts on transport use by both officers and customers;

- Economic development activities need to recognise the environmental effects of different kinds and locations of development;

- One department's 'efficiency gain' should not be bought at the expense of extra costs or service reductions elsewhere. For example, abolishing central purchasing advice and control can mean that appraisal of the environmental impact of products and research into environmentally better methods has to be duplicated - or ceases to be done at all.

Integrating sustainable development aims into the local authority's policies and activities

Green housekeeping. An authority can improve its own direct effects on the environment through:

- Energy conservation in its own buildings;

- Restriction of car allowances and leases to those operationally necessary, and phasing out car perks and subsidies such as higher payments for more wasteful cars and free commuter parking;

- Green transport incentives, such as cycle and public transport allowances, cycle parking, changing and showering;

- Waste minimisation, reuse and recycling, for example of office paper;

- Purchasing policies to minimise quantities, base specifications on fitness for purpose, durability, avoid 'gold plating' and give preference to environmentally better options.

All policies and services have environmental and development effects, which can be improved. Some of the most important follow.

Land use planning. New government guidance (in the new set of Planning Policy Guidance Notes or PPGs) sanctions and encourages authorities to promote sustainability through the planning system. Subject to the views of Inspectors (who sometimes seem not to have read the new PPGs!) policies in structure plans and local plans can seek to:

- Promote development which reduces the need to travel (for example by resisting out-of-town retail developments);

- Encourage resource- and energy-efficient patterns of development;

- Favour sustainability-enhancing developments such as wind farms;

- Constrain development within natural 'carrying capacity' limits and locally adopted environmental quality objectives (although government targets for aggregate extraction and housing are still imposed without reference to environmental capacities);

- Protect habitats and landscapes - not only rare and 'critical' ones.

Development control and building control activities can encourage energy-efficient and environmentally benign building practices through design guidance.

Transport policies and programmes can

- Take access to amenities rather than mobility in itself as their overall aim;

- Seek to reduce the need to travel;

- Promote and facilitate walking, cycling and public transport;

- Encourage a shift away from car use towards less environmentally damaging modes;

Economic development activities can:

- Advise local businesses on improving environmental performance (as part of general business management advice);

- Encourage environmentally beneficial choice and management of sites and buildings;

- Provide sustainability-enhancing infrastructure such as public transport, cycle routes, recycling and waste heat distribution;

- Set (realistic) environmental management criteria for grant and support schemes;

- Proactively develop and encourage environmental businesses.

Tendering and purchaser/provider splits. Environmental criteria can be applied to tenders provided they relate to the goods or services being bought (rather than the suppliers' other activities) and are not 'anticompetitive'. DoE has given helpful guidance on interpreting 'anticompetitive' in the Eco-Management and Audit Guide (see sources of further information).

Housing services can build and refurbish to high standards of energy efficiency, and take advantage of the Homes Energy Efficiency Scheme to provide energy advice, insulation and draughtproofing for tenants.

Tourism and visitor strategies can encourage 'green tourism', provide and promote sustainable tourism infrastructure such as public transport and cycle routes and promote environmental management by hotels, guest houses and such like.

Health strategies can emphasise the environmental / lifestyle dimension of health, and the role of environmental changes such as reductions in traffic and car use in increasing health.

Welfare, equal opportunities and poverty strategies can recognise the linkages between economic, social and environmental deprivation, and use them to solve problems. For example:

- Fuel poverty can be tackled through improving the energy efficiency of low-income housing;

- Better public transport increases the ability of disadvantaged people to access amenities, and may reduce car use and thus the health and amenity damage which they suffer from traffic.

Explicitly 'environmental' services. Authorities can develop sustainability-related strategies and work programmes for a range of explicitly environmental topics including:

- Recycling and waste minimisation (minimisation should take priority);

- Nature conservation and wildlife protection;

- Landscape;

- Leisure and recreation (which should emphasise environmentally benign activities and means of transport).

Action in the Wider Community

The key to Local Agenda 21 - what makes it more than just a collection of environmental initiatives at local level - is the ideal of actively involving the local community in working together towards sustainable development. Local authorities can initiate and facilitate four kinds of action to achieve this: awareness raising and education; consulting and involving the general public; partnerships with groups within the local community; and measuring, monitoring and reporting on progress towards sustainability.

Awareness raising and education

To have an effective voice in decision making, people have to know what the issues and the constraints are, and have to undertand the impact their own lifestyles have. Possible actions to support this include:

*   **Support for environmental education** in schools and colleges - for example through provision of resource centres and specialist advisers;

*   **Awareness-raising events,** for example in Environment Week;

*   Schools **visits and talks** to local clubs and societies;

*   **Support for voluntary groups'** information activities;

*   **Publication of local environmental information,** such as State of the Environment reporting and levels of sustainability indicators (see below) and statements on the authority's own environmental policies and performance (see environmental management systems, above);

*   **Press releases** on significant developments in the local environment.

Individuals will be motivated to act if they can see how their own behaviour can help solve environmental and development problems. Awareness initiatives should emphasise:

*   The connections between our behaviour - as consumers, residents, workers, tourists and so on - and sustainability issues;

*   The opportunities for **practical action** and **behaviour change.**

Consulting and involving the general public

Sustainable development requires that objectives for environmental quality should guide policy at all levels from global to local. These objectives should be set by open and democratic processes. Both traditional and novel methods of consultation and involvement can help achieve this.

Public consultation processes are already required by law, or are standard practice, for a range of local authority functions such as development plan reviews. Local Agenda 21 implies that this kind of consultation should be:

*   Aimed at all the community;

*   Carried out whenever important questions of environmental objectives arise, and not only when statutorily required;

*   Physically accessible (through such means as touring exhibitions, walk-in caravans etc);

*   Accessible also in the broader sense of clear, simple, attractive and unintimidating presentation so that the widest range of people can contribute their views;

*   Given considerable weight in decision taking.

Even at their best, traditional consultation methods will have trouble reaching the less articulate and confident - and the less mobile and 'pushy'. The following newer methods can help.

Fora. Some UK local authorities have helped establish Environmental Fora or Local Agenda 21 Fora where a range of organisations and interests can discuss and propose solutions to environmental problems. Different groups - business, environmental, womens', ethnic, occupational, campaigning, area-based or leisure interest - can all bring their own perspectives and contributions. 'Forum' can also mean a more specialised group. For example the National Recycling Forum brings together local authorities, businesses and environmental groups to work on policies and projects in recycling and waste minimisation.

Focus groups, where six to eight people with particular characteristics (for example members of ethnic groups, or people without cars, or on low incomes) are invited and helped by a facilitator to discuss their views on selected topics - for example provision of public transport. Focus groups will not produce statistically representative views. But they can reach minority groups and get a deeper and more illuminating response than traditional survey techniques.

'Planning for real' exercises, where again small groups of people, with expert facilitators 'on tap not on top', try out different approaches to real planning problems affecting their own lives, often using pictures or models rather than words. The advantages are immediacy, practicality, and accessibility.

'Parish Maps', where local people (individuals, established environmental, local history, or social groups, or a new grouping) produce a map of what they value about their local community and its surroundings. The process of making a parish map should stimulate discussion about what makes a place particular and different and it should serve as a reminder of what local people value, so that these features are not lost. The creation of a parish map should be the starting point for creating awareness about the local environment and lead on to action, not be an end in itself.

Feedback mechanisms such as Global Action Plan or Ecofeedback can help involve individuals and families in monitoring and improving their own environmental imapact in their daily lives.

These can be combined with traditional consultation methods involving Parish Councils, Town Councils, residents' associations and other 'grass roots' bodies. These should be supported and treated as partners in decision taking.

*P*artnerships with groups within the local community

Local authorities should work with other organisations and interest groups on sustainability issues in general and on specific projects and initiatives.

Meetings, workshops and conferences can be held on a one-off basis to involve a range of interests in specific decisions, and 'test the water' for more established collaboration.

Working Groups / advisory groups. Many authorities involve local business and / or environmental groups in standing working groups or advisory groups on environmental topics, working with officers, and sometimes members too, to develop new environmental policies. They can:

• Help find methods which have community support;

• Secure support for new departures;

• Help partners learn from each other's experience.

Round Tables. This is a term now being applied so widely that it is in danger of becoming just another name for seminar or workshop! This would be a pity since it would lose the very useful and distinctive meanings the term has developed in Canada. Canadian Round Tables are:

• Standing bodies, not one-off meetings;

• Composed of senior representatives of government, business and environmental interests;

• Active at a wide range of scales: there is a national Round Table, one in each Province, and many in individual cities and towns;

• Non-hierarchical, and meeting on terms of equality - not 'owned' or dominated by any one partner;

- Serviced by a staff secretariat (usually provided by one of the partners), and with (limited) funds to commission research and produce publications;

- Without direct executive powers, but enjoying high prestige and influence, and often consulted on or asked to propose policies and initiatives - in other words, not just talking - shops;

- Able to set up specialist subgroups.

The Environment City model. In the UK the Environment City programme run by the RSNC Wildlife Trusts Partnership has many similarities to the Canadian model, but some differences:

- The Environment City 'round tables' do have executive power;

- The model operates at the city-wide level, not county or regional;

- Community representatives are included.

Partnership initiatives can also run more specifically defined initiatives and practical projects:

- The Energy Action Cities, Recycling Cities and Environment Cities are all partnerships between local authorities, businesses and environmental bodies to run coordinated area-based environmental programmes;

- Local authorities can work with local businesses to deliver economic, social and environmental objectives together, for example in energy efficiency work or physical environmental improvements;

- Local authorities can set up partnerships to harness business expertise and investment for projects such as combined heat and power or recycling facilities;

- Partnerships between farmers, landowners and conservation groups can safeguard, improve or create wildlife habitats.

Developing-world partnerships and support. Local authorities and communities can develop partnerships with local authorities in the developing world to share experience. Developing countries can benefit greatly from access to skills and resources from the

'developed' world. But the benefits are not just one way: the UK now shares many 'developing world' problems such as urban poverty, deprivation, begging, malnutrition and pollution, and we can learn many lessons from the developing world in dealing with them.

All these provide a framework for different interests to work together, over time, to agree on problems and objectives, and develop solutions. The aim is to break down the barriers of distrust and conflict of interest by giving participants better understanding of each others' problems, and joint 'ownership' of the solutions. Another term for this approach is **multistakeholder partnerships.**

Measuring, monitoring and reporting on progress towards sustainability

Environmental objectives, and actions in pursuit of sustainable development, must be based on knowledge and understanding of how our actions are threatening sustainability. Defining, collecting and sharing information about this should therefore form part of a Local Agenda 21 process. A number of techniques can help.

Environmental monitoring. Local authorities and local groups can contribute to understanding of global environmental change by taking part in national and international programmes of monitoring of (for example) air pollution or species diversity.

Local state of the environment reporting. Local authorities and local groups can carry out detailed surveys of the state of the local environment. These can be a valuable educational and promotional tool - particularly if local people and organisations are involved, for example through 'parish mapping' exercises and schools projects.

They can also help guide decisions on priority actions, particularly if information is collected repeatedly to build up a picture of change. Care must be taken to avoid wasting time and money collecting information which will not have any practical use. Through its 'stewardship' role, the local authority will already have access to much relevant information, and has an obligation under the European Union's Directive on the freedom of access to information on the environment (90/313/EEC) to provide public access to environmental information.

Sustainability indicators are measurable features which tell us whether we are getting more or less sustainable. Indicators must:

- be significant;

- have a reasoned relationship to sustainability at both global and local level;

- be relevant to local government, but also to the ordinary citizen (ie not performance indicators for local authorities, but for local communities);

- reflect local circumstances;

- be based on (relatively) easy to collect information;

- show trends over reasonable timescales;

- have a relationship to other sets of indicators;

- be both individually and collectively meaningful;

- be clear, easy to understand and educate as well as inform;

- provoke changes (in policies, services, lifestyles and so on);

- lead to the setting of targets or thresholds.

Targets. Indicators articulate values and aspirations, and thus help set the policy agenda. But they only change our behaviour when we set targets for rates of change or for particular levels to be reached by specified times. (The environmental management systems mentioned above require specific targets to be set for each action - both to make sure the action gets carried out and to see if it is effective at producing the desired results).

Environmental Impact Assessment (EIA) provides information - an Environmental

Statement - about how a proposed project or development will change the environment. Local authorities can:

- Carry out, and publish, assessments for all their own projects;

- Set guidelines for environmental statements to ensure they give adequate coverage to important issues. Environmental statements are required by law for many large projects. But the assessments are done by consultants chosen and paid by the developers, and there are few standards or safeguards for coverage or quality;

- Give environmental statements high prominence in planning and other development decisions.

A limitation of EIA is that it comes too late in the decision process. Once there is a project proposal on which an assessment can be carried out - for example to build a road - it will often be too late to look at alternatives (such as different transport or planning policies which avoid the need for the road), and the assessment will only be able to suggest 'mitigation' of environmental impacts (such as nice landscaping).

Strategic environmental assessment - that is, assessment of the impacts of policies, programmes and plans, and consideration of alternative ways of achieving objectives before any specific projects are under discussion - is intended to avoid this problem. The European Union has proposed that it should be standard practice. Methods for it are being developed, and can be applied by local authorities.

WORKING TOWARDS LOCAL AGENDA 21

A Local Agenda 21 process should start from a commitment to sustainability and should involve progress in each of the six areas of action set out above.

To give the process structure and momentum it may be helpful to aim for the production of a local strategy for sustainable development by 1996, the deadline given in Agenda 21. This could:

- Be a short, clear and accessible published document;

- Identify the main sustainability issues and aims for the area;

- Contain explicit objectives for both the state of the environment and for indicators of the quality of life in the area;

- Say which organisations or sectors will take what actions (and by when) to work towards these objectives - and how performance and achievements will be assessed;

- Set out a review process for the whole programme.

The Local Agenda 21 Steering Group invites every local authority in the UK to send the Local Agenda 21 Project Officer by the end of 1996:

- a local strategy or action plan for sustainable development;

- a short report outlining its progress in the six areas described above.

APPENDIX: SOURCES OF FURTHER INFORMATION

All the priced LGMB publications mentioned below are available from: Publications Unit, Local Government Management Board, Arndale House, Arndale Centre, Luton LU1 2TS. For free of charge LGMB publications write to Glenna Johnson, Environment Unit, LGMB.

International and national policy background

Agenda 21, United Nations 1992, available from United Nations Association. Agenda 21 itself is hard to read. For most purposes it is easier to use one of two shorter and more digestible summaries:

- *Agenda 21: a Guide for Local Authorities in the UK*, LGMB, 1992 (specifically covers local authority interests), free of charge.

- *A Plain Language Guide to Agenda 21*, (broader), 1992, Centre For Our Common Future, Palais Wilson, 52 rue des Paquis, 1201 Geneva, tel: 010 41 22 732 7117.

Fifth Environmental Action Programme, Commission of the European Communities, Brussels, 1992. Available from HMSO. As with Agenda 21, the LGMB has produced a handy Guide to the Programme (free of charge).

A Framework for Local Sustainability, LGMB, 1993, £15: a detailed statement of local government's interpretation of sustainable development and what it requires of both local and national government, endorsed by all the UK local authority associations. A more worked - out version of the *Initial Statement*, which it supersedes. Includes the *UK Local Government Declaration on Sustainable Development*.

UK Local Government Declaration on Sustainable Development, LGMB, 1993, free of charge: a short statement of principle endorsed by all the UK local authority associations.

Sustainable Development: the UK Strategy, HMSO, 1994: the 'official' Government view. Criticised by many environmentalists for lacking concrete commitments to action, it is nevertheless a huge advance in policy thinking.

Canadian Round Tables and Other Mechanisms for Sustainable Development in Canada, LGMB, 1994, £5.

Guidance on local authority good practice in general

The Friends of the Earth Environmental Charter for Local Government, 1989, FoE, 26-28 Underwood Street, London N1 7JQ, tel: 071 490 1555. Pioneering guide which was very influential in setting the sustainability agenda, and is still highly relevant.

Environmental Practice Guide, second edition, LGMB, 1992, £25: major collection of examples of local authority activities and initiatives.

Greening Your Local Authority, ed. Janice Morphet, Longman, to be published during 1994: practical guide with chapters on many of the topics discussed above.

Stepping Stones - the BT Environment City Review of Sustainability, 1993, RSNC Wildlife Trusts Partnership, The Green, Whitham Park, Waterside South, Lincoln LN5 7JR, tel: 0522 544400. A selection of pioneering projects from around the world, concentrating on the four UK Environment Cities.

Guidance on specific tools and activities

A Guide to the Eco-Management and Audit Scheme for UK Local Government, HMSO, 1993. Detailed guide to applying the management systems approach to a local authority. Can also be used for BS7750 or for simply 'brushing up' parts of a management system.